RHINO

by **CAROLINE ARNOLD**
photographs by **RICHARD HEWETT**
with additional photographs by **ARTHUR P. ARNOLD**

Morrow Junior Books • New York

PHOTO CREDITS: Photographs by Arthur P. Arnold: pages 1, 4–5, 6, 7, 16 (bottom), 21, 22, 24–25, 26, 27, 30, 35, 39, 41, 44, 46–47.

The text type is 14-point Caslon 224 Book.

Library of Congress Cataloging-in-Publication Data   Arnold, Caroline.   Rhino/by Caroline Arnold; photographs by Richard Hewett, with additional photographs by Arthur P. Arnold.   p.   cm.   ISBN 0-688-12694-4 (trade)—ISBN 0-688-12695-2 (library)   1. Rhinoceroses—Juvenile literature.   [1. Rhinoceroses.]   I. Hewett, Richard, ill.   II. Arnold, Arthur, ill.   III. Title.   QL737.U63A7   1995   599.72'8—dc20   94-23904   CIP   AC

ACKNOWLEDGMENTS

Umfulozi and Kruger are white rhinos that originally came from South Africa to the Whipsnade Zoo in England in the 1970s as part of a program to establish breeding groups of white rhinos in zoos outside of Africa. At the same time, another group of white rhinos went to the San Diego Wild Animal Park in California. In both groups, the rhinos mated and have produced many babies. Forty-six zoos in the United States and Canada currently have white rhinos on exhibit. All of the photos in this book are of white rhinos except for the one of the Indian rhino above and where noted in the captions. Several zoos in the United States, including the Los Angeles, Cincinnati, and Bronx zoos, are also participating in captive breeding programs for black, Indian, and Sumatran rhinos.

We would like to thank the Edinburgh Zoo in Scotland for the opportunity to photograph their white rhinos. We also thank John Cousens of Edinburgh for his kind help. For additional photographs of rhinos, we are grateful to Wildlife Safari in Winston, Oregon, and to the Los Angeles Zoo in California for their cooperation in this project. And, as always, we thank our editor, Andrea Curley, for her continued support.

AT THE ZOO

It was a bright, clear morning, and Shimba, a three-week-old rhinoceros, was full of energy. While her mother and father watched, she cantered across the open space of their enclosure, her tiny hooves digging into the soft dirt. Although she did not yet have horns on her face, by the time she was full grown she would have two long horns just like those of her parents. With their thick horns, large heads, and massive bodies, rhinoceroses look something like living armored tanks. They are one of the most unusual-looking animals—and among the most endangered. By learning more about them, we can find out how to help them and protect the wild places where they live.

Shimba and her parents are white rhinoceroses that live at the Edinburgh Zoo in Edinburgh, Scotland. Shimba and the other rhinos are comfortable at the zoo. They get good care from the keepers and have a large outdoor enclosure with plenty of room to move around. At night and in cold or rainy weather, they can go inside a barn.

Shimba is named after an area in South Africa where rhinos and other wild animals live. Shimba's mother is called Umfulozi, and her father is called Kruger, after the names of two wild animal reserves in South Africa. These reserves were established about 100 years ago in order to protect rhinoceroses from hunters. Kruger and Umfulozi were born in South Africa in 1969 and came to Great Britain in the early 1970s. They have lived at the Edinburgh Zoo since May 1976. They mated for the first time soon after arriving in Scotland and have produced a new baby rhino about every two years since then. Shimba is their eighth baby.

RHINOS IN DANGER

Breeding rhinos in captivity is one of the ways that people are trying to save rhinos from extinction. Caring for rhinos in zoos and wild animal parks also provides opportunities for people to observe these huge animals up close.

Wild rhinos are endangered chiefly because people kill them for their valuable horns. Traditional medical practices in many African and Asian countries use ground-up rhino horns to treat illnesses. In some Middle Eastern countries, rhino horns are highly prized for making the handles of special daggers called *djambias*. Rhino horns are so valuable that poachers, or illegal hunters, continue to kill rhinoceroses even though it is against the law. In many of the remote places where rhinos live, it is difficult to enforce the laws that protect them. Rhinos are also endangered where their habitat has been destroyed for farms and ranches.

The outlook for wild rhinos today is bleak. As long as rhino horn is in demand for medicines and other uses, the animals are in danger. People are trying to help rhinos in several ways. These include captive breeding; protecting them better from poachers; preserving their natural habitat; and in some cases, moving them to new, safer locations. In Africa, wildlife managers are also trying another idea. To make these animals less attractive to poachers, they are catching the rhinos and removing their horns. Then they are letting the animals go. This procedure does not hurt the rhinos and may save their lives.

Scientists are studying rhinos both in the wild and in captivity. As they learn more about what rhinos eat, how they reproduce, and the ways in which they behave, they will be better able to help them survive.

PREHISTORIC RHINOS

People have been fascinated by rhinoceroses since prehistoric times. In ancient Persia, cups were carved from rhino horn more than 2,500 years ago. Ancient Romans put a live rhinoceros on exhibition. When Marco Polo traveled to Sumatra in the 1300s, he saw a rhino for the first time. He thought that the strange beast with a horn in the middle of its face must be a unicorn, an animal made popular in myths and legends. But unlike unicorns, which are imaginary, rhinos are real animals that have lived on earth for millions of years.

The first rhinoceroses lived about 40 million years ago in Europe, Africa, Asia, and North America. Fossil bones found in these places show that there were more than thirty species, or kinds, of prehistoric rhinos. They varied in size and appearance and were adapted to a wide range of diets and habitats. Some prehistoric rhinoceroses had no horns, while others had several. The animals ranged in size

from only 2 feet (.61 meter) tall to a huge animal called *Indricotherium,* which was 18 feet (5.5 meters) tall and weighed 33 tons (30 metric tons). This rhino had no horns and only four teeth. *Indricotherium* is also called *Baluchitherium,* after the state in Pakistan where its huge fossil bones were found. It is the heaviest land mammal that ever lived.

Rhinos became extinct in North America about 5 million years ago, but in Europe they existed until the end of the last Ice Age, about 10,000 years ago. The woolly rhinos of Europe were hunted by Stone Age people, who drew pictures of them on cave walls in southern France 30,000 years ago. The woolly rhinoceros was 11 feet (3.4 meters) long and had two large horns. Its shaggy coat and large size helped it to survive in the cold climate of the Ice Age. Preserved bodies of woolly rhinos have been found in frozen ground in Siberia and in bogs in Europe.

RHINOS TODAY

Today, there are five species of rhinoceroses. The white and black rhinos live in Africa. The Indian, Javan, and Sumatran rhinos are found in Asia. Although the five species of rhinos vary somewhat in their appearance and behavior, they share many characteristics, including their unique facial horns and their enormous body size.

There are two subspecies of **white rhinos,** the northern and southern, and both are found in the open grassland of Africa. Until recently, northern white rhinos lived in central Africa in Uganda, Zaire, and the southern part of Sudan. Today this subspecies is in great danger of becoming extinct because poachers have killed nearly all of these animals. Now northern white rhinos are found only in a national park in Zaire, where there are fewer than 100 of them. Nearly 6,000 southern white rhinos live in South Africa. This subspecies was nearly wiped out by hunters at the end of the nineteenth century, but the government established a number of reserves where the rhinos could live safely, and their number has gradually increased.

The name *white rhino* is misleading because this rhino's skin is actually gray. *White* comes from the Dutch word *widje,* which means "wide mouth." (Dutch traders and farmers who came to South Africa in the 1600s used this word to describe the rhinoceroses they saw.) The white rhino is also sometimes called the square-lipped rhino because of its broad mouth.

White rhinos are the largest rhino species and, along with hippopotamuses, are the second largest land animal. (Elephants are the largest.) An adult male white rhino stands up to 7 feet (2.1 meters) tall at the shoulder and can weigh up to 10,000 pounds (4,545.5 kilograms). Female white rhinos are slightly smaller. A small hump behind the white rhino's head is formed by strong muscles at the top of the shoulders.

White rhino.

White rhinos are the only rhino species that forms social groups. In the wild, females and their young often live in herds of up to six animals. Usually these are family groups of related animals. Adult males live alone and establish territories. Although a male white rhino may go into other males' territories, he only mates in his own. Female white rhinos do not have territories. They move about freely in search of food.

Black rhino (opposite and above).

Most **black rhinos** live in East Africa south of the Sahara Desert, although a few are found in West and central Africa. Black rhinos are sometimes seen in open country, but they usually live in areas covered by bushes and trees. Both male and female black rhinos are solitary and live alone most of the time.

About 2,000 black rhinos live in the wild. In recent years they have disappeared from many of the places where they formerly lived. The few black rhinos that remain are seriously endangered.

The black rhino is about 5 feet (1.52 meters) tall at the shoulder and weighs about 2,500 pounds (1,136.4 kilograms). Its gray skin is slightly darker than that of the white rhino. The black rhino is sometimes called the hook-lipped rhino because of its pointed upper lip, which can be used to grasp food. The shapes of their mouths easily distinguish black rhinos from white rhinos. Black rhinos are also smaller than white rhinos, have rounder ears, and have no shoulder hump. Both white and black rhinos have two horns.

Indian rhino.

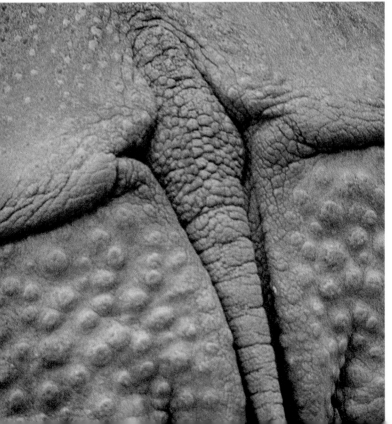

Indian rhino skin.

The **Indian rhino** is found only in Nepal and in northeastern India. Including those in zoos, there are fewer than 2,000 Indian rhinos in the world. Their habitat includes swampy areas surrounded by dense, 12-foot- (3.7-meter-) high elephant grass.

The large size and knobby skin of the Indian rhino make it look as if it were wearing a suit of armor. In the wild, tough skin protects the Indian rhino as it moves through thorny thickets. The skin is stiff and folded over the shoulders and hindquarters. Where it is folded, the skin is thinner and more flexible, so the rhino can move more easily. The Indian rhino stands 6 feet (1.83 meters) high or more at the shoulder and can weigh as much as 9,000 pounds (4,090.9 kilograms). It has just one horn.

The **Javan rhino** is similar in appearance to the Indian rhino but is somewhat smaller. It is about 5 feet (1.52 meters) tall and weighs about 4,000 pounds (1,818.2 kilograms). The skin of the Javan rhino is folded like that of the Indian rhino, but instead of round bumps, the Javan rhino's skin is marked with a series of intersecting cracks that form a cross-hatched pattern. Javan rhinos live in dense tropical forests on the island of Java in the South Pacific and in South Vietnam. They are the rarest of all rhinos and the species in most danger of extinction. There are no captive Javan rhinos and only about sixty live in the wild. Most live in the Udjong Kulon Reserve in western Java.

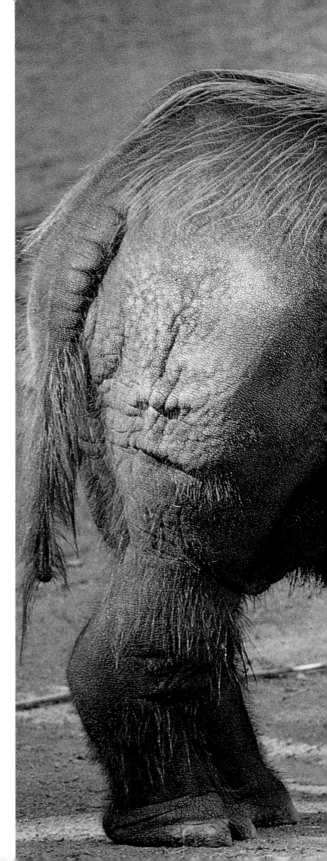

A young Sumatran rhino.

The **Sumatran rhino,** also called the **Asian hairy rhino,** lives on the islands of Sumatra and Borneo and in parts of Malaysia. It is at home in lowland tropical rain forests as well as on wooded mountain slopes. The Sumatran rhino is distinguished by coarse reddish brown hair along its back and sides and long tufts of black hair on the tips of its ears. Unlike the other Asian rhinos, it has two horns.

The Sumatran rhino is the smallest of all the rhino species. An adult Sumatran rhino is about 4 feet (1.2 meters) tall at the shoulder and weighs about 1,850 pounds (840.9 kilograms). Scientists believe that the Sumatran rhino is the direct descendant of the extinct woolly rhinos that roamed Europe thousands of years ago. About 800 Sumatran rhinos live in the wild. Four zoos in the United States are working with the Indonesian government to establish a breeding program in captivity for these extremely endangered animals.

"NOSE HORN"

The name *rhinoceros* comes from two Greek words meaning "nose horn." The distinguishing feature of rhinoceroses is that they have one or two large horns growing on the front of the face. The longest known rhino horn was more than 5 feet (1.5 meters) long!

The horn at the front of the nose is usually larger than the one behind it. (Occasionally rhinos do not grow horns, and some black rhinoceroses have small horny knobs in addition to their horns.) African rhinos have longer horns than Asian rhinos. Shorter horns may make it easier for the Asian rhinos to move through the dense jungles in which they live.

A rhino's horn is made of a hard substance called keratin, the same material that forms fingernails. On a rhino the keratin grows in long hair-like strands to form layers that make a strong, solid horn.

A newborn rhino has no horn, but a patch of smooth skin covers the place where the horn will grow. The horn starts to grow when the rhino is about five weeks old. At first it looks like a round knob; by the time a white rhino baby is five months old, the horn is about 1½ inches (3.8 centimeters) long. A rhino's horn grows throughout its life and can increase as much as 3 inches (7.7 centimeters) each year. If the horn breaks off, it will grow back.

Rhinos use their horns to fight one another and to fend off attackers. The horn is used as a club or a spike, and its sharp point can inflict a deep wound. A rhino uses its strong neck muscles to thrust its horn into an opponent. The horn can also be used to hook an object and fling it into the air. Rhinos sometimes dig holes in the ground with their horns. Scientists think that they may do this to find salt and other minerals that they need in their diet.

FAMILY LIFE

A female rhino is called a *cow*. Although she is able to mate for the first time when she is between three and five years old, a female does not usually mate and produce a baby until she is about six. After that, she has a new baby every two or three years.

Male rhinos are called *bulls*. They can mate for the first time between the ages of five and eight, but in the wild, most do not have the chance to mate until they are about twelve. By then, they have grown to their full size and strength. Males often fight one another for the chance to mate with a female, so the strongest males do most of the mating. A male can detect when a female is ready to mate by her smell. Mating can take place at any time of year. A rhino male does not stay with the female after mating and does not help care for the baby rhino after it is born.

The length of time that a female rhinoceros is pregnant varies among the five species, ranging from about 240 days for the Sumatran rhino to 517 days for the white rhino. A rhino mother gives birth to a single baby, which is called a *calf*. (In rare cases, rhinos have given birth to twins.)

Rhino calves vary greatly in size, depending on the species. A white rhino calf weighs about 110 pounds (50 kilograms) at birth, whereas a black rhino weighs only 44 pounds (20 kilograms). Newborn Asian rhino calves range from 51 to 165 pounds (23.2 to 75 kilograms) in weight.

Soon after Shimba was born, her mother licked her clean. A newborn rhino is well developed and able to stand within an hour of its birth. As soon as it is on its feet, it nudges under its mother's belly to find one of her two teats.

Like other mammals, a baby rhino drinks its mother's milk. A wild rhino calf begins to eat plants when it is about a week old, but it continues to nurse until it is one to two years old. At the zoo, Shimba began to nibble pieces of hay when she was about three weeks old.

Shimba grew quickly, and by two months old she weighed 150 pounds (68.2 kilograms). By the time Shimba is a year old, she will weigh more than 1,000 pounds (454.5 kilograms). She will not be fully grown until she is about five years old or more. Male rhinos reach their adult size somewhat later than females.

In the wild, a young rhino stays with its mother until just before the next calf is born. Usually this occurs when the young rhino is about three years old. By then, it can take care of itself. A young female white rhino may join her mother's herd. A male rhino goes off by himself. Shimba will be separated from her parents before Umfulozi has another calf.

A rhino mother usually keeps her new calf hidden for several weeks until it is strong enough to follow her easily. A young rhino stays close to its mother as she moves about to feed. A black rhino mother usually walks behind her youngster, whereas a white rhino mother typically leads her calf.

Because of their size, adult rhinos are safe from all predators except humans. Young rhinos, on the other hand, are sometimes attacked by wild animals. Lions, hyenas, crocodiles, and tigers prey on young rhino calves.

A mother rhinoceros watches over her youngster closely and charges any animal that comes too near. At the zoo, Umfulozi guarded Shimba carefully and, at first, did not even let her go near Kruger. If Shimba wandered too close to her father, Umfulozi quickly moved between them. In the wild, a mother white rhino waits until her calf is several weeks old before they rejoin the herd.

THE SENSES

A rhinoceros does not see well and cannot identify objects at a distance. Because its eyes are on either side of its head, it cannot focus on things that are straight ahead. Instead, the rhino turns its head from side to side and looks out of one eye at a time.

A rhino's sense of hearing is excellent, and it can rotate its ears to locate sounds precisely. Rhinos use a variety of sounds to communicate with one another. Fighting rhinos grunt and scream. Males and females whistle to each other before mating. If a mother and her calf become separated, they call to each other with soft mewing sounds. Recently, scientists discovered that rhinos often communicate with sounds so low that humans cannot hear them. These extremely low sounds, which are called infrasounds, travel well over long distances and allow the animals to "talk" even when they cannot see one another.

The sense of smell is also extremely important for rhinos. Mothers and calves can recognize each other by their odors, and young rhinos learn to identify smells in their surroundings. Rhinos can smell a predator from up to half a mile (.8 kilometer) away. Big nostrils and unusually large cavities inside the nose help give rhinos their keen sense of smell.

Rhinos can detect the presence of other rhinos by the scent of their urine and dung. Males spray urine to mark their territories, and females spray to show they are ready to mate. Rhinos also mark their territories with dung. They make large piles of dung and trample them with their feet. As rhinos walk through their territory, they leave trails of scent.

Indian rhino.

All rhinoceroses have thick tough skin that protects them from sharp twigs and thorns when they are walking through dense vegetation. With the exception of the Sumatran rhino, which is hairy all over, rhinos are hairless except on the ears and the tip of the tail. (Newborn rhinos of other species sometimes have hair, but it falls out by the time the calf is one year old.)

The tail is between 25 and 30 inches (64.1–76.9 centimeters) long, depending on the rhino's age and species. The stiff hairs at the end help make it a good flyswatter. When a rhino is alarmed, it curls its tail in a corkscrew shape.

In the wild, birds sometimes perch on the backs of rhinos. The birds eat insects crawling on the rhinos' skin. Even though a rhino's skin is thick, the rhino can feel a bird on its back. It can also hear the bird, and if the bird calls out or flies away, the rhino knows that another animal may be near. This alerts the rhino to possible danger.

Rhinos like to roll in dirt or mud to protect their skin from the sun and from biting insects. Wet mud also helps a rhino to cool off when the weather is hot. Another way that rhinos keep cool is by sweating, and on hot days moisture may pour down their skin. At the zoo, rain puddles made good places for the rhinos to take mud baths. In the wild, rhinos often go to the edges of ponds and streams to wallow.

Rhinos sometimes rub against trees or other large objects to scratch themselves. When a rhino rubs, it leaves some of its scent behind, and this tells other rhinos that it has been there.

At the zoo, several logs in the rhinos' enclosure made good scratching posts. Rhinos in captivity also seem to enjoy having their backs scratched by their keepers. Except when they are alarmed, rhinos are usually gentle animals. Even so, keepers in zoos are always careful when they work with large animals like rhinoceroses.

FOOD AND WATER

A rhino has a huge appetite to match its large size. In captivity, a full-grown white rhino can eat 50 pounds (22.7 kilograms) or more of food each day. Rhinos are plant eaters, and their flexible necks and long heads help them reach their food. A rhino's diet depends on its species and habitat. The white rhino has a mouth that is especially well suited to eating grass. The rhino grazes low to the ground and uses its wide lips to clip off blades of grass like a lawn mower. Keepers at the zoo feed Shimba and the other rhinos a variety of fresh vegetables, hay, and vitamin pellets.

All other species of rhinoceroses are browsers, that is, animals that feed on the leaves and branches of larger plants. Black rhinos eat the shoots and twigs of low-growing bushes. Occasionally they also eat fruit. A black rhino uses its flexible upper lip to grasp pieces of food and pull them into its mouth.

Indian rhinos eat young grass, twigs, and plants that grow in the swampy areas where they live.

Both Javan and Sumatran rhinos are forest dwellers. The Javan rhino mainly eats young trees, using its body to bend them until they break and fall over. Then it eats the leaves at the top. Sumatran rhinos eat branches and shoots, leaves, fruits, lichens, and fungi.

Rhinos have from twenty-four to thirty-four teeth, depending on their species. Neither white nor black rhinos have front teeth. Instead, they use their lips to break off the plants they eat. Asian rhinos, on the other hand, have sharp front teeth, including long tusklike canine teeth, which they use when fighting. All rhino species have strong molar teeth in the back of the mouth, which they use to crush and chew food.

Rhinos need to drink water regularly. Drinking replenishes water that is lost by urinating and sweating. In the wild, rhinos go to a water hole or river to drink every few days. Rhinos usually stay within a day's walk from a source of water. During extended dry periods, large numbers of rhinos may gather around a few water holes. When water is scarce, rhinos may use their front feet to dig holes in dry riverbeds to find water below the surface. At the zoo, the rhinos always have clean drinking water in a trough.

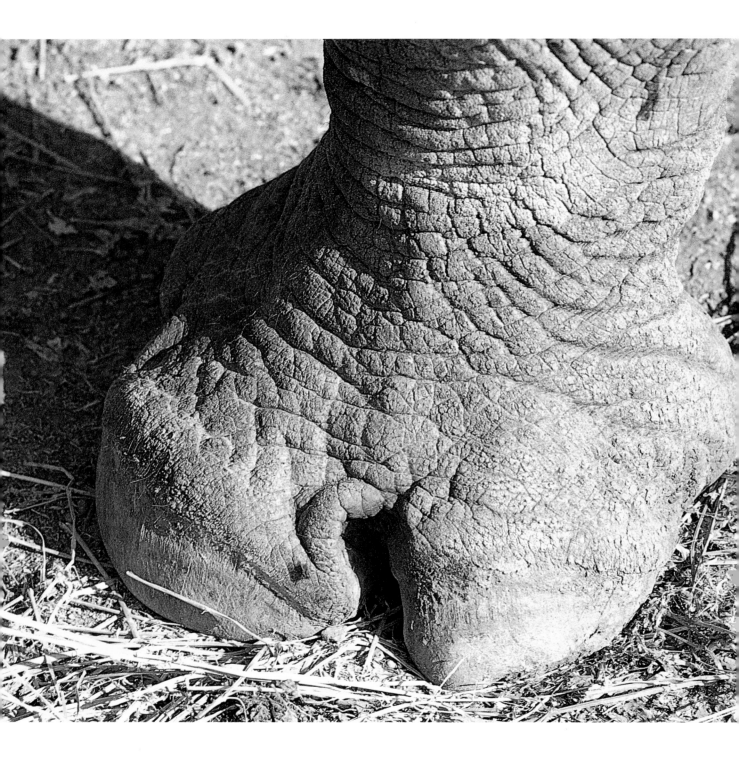

MOVING ABOUT

Rhinoceroses belong to the scientific order called Perissodactyla, a name that comes from Greek words meaning "odd fingered." Horses and tapirs are also in this order. All of the animals in this group have three toes and use the middle toe to support the body's weight. (With horses, the side toes have disappeared and the middle toe is greatly enlarged.) These animals never place the heel of the foot on the ground. Instead, they always walk on tiptoe.

A rhino's foot is about 12 inches (30.8 centimeters) wide. As with horses and tapirs, a rhino's feet are adapted for running, with a thick hoof protecting the bottom of each toe. When rhinos are kept in zoos, they cannot wear down their hooves as they would in the wild. Therefore, the keepers sometimes have to trim their hooves. This painless procedure is similar to cutting fingernails.

Rhinos are agile animals and can move quickly despite their large size. The trotting speed of a rhino is about 18 miles (29 kilometers) per hour, but for short distances rhinos can run at speeds of 25 miles (40 kilometers) per hour or more. A typical walking speed is 3 miles (4.8 kilometers) per hour.

41

Indian rhinos (above and opposite).

Most Indian rhinos live in swampy areas and bathe daily. The pools where Indian rhinos bathe are usually surrounded by jungle. As the rhinos push their way through the thick plants to the water, they make paths that other animals can also use. The Javan rhino is a good swimmer and sometimes even goes into the ocean.

In the wild, rhinos frequently go into water to cool off. In zoos, they often have pools for swimming, and keepers sometimes hose them off as well.

Like other young animals, rhino calves are curious about their surroundings. As Shimba explored, she stopped to touch and smell things. She also seemed to enjoy running about the enclosure, an exercise that helped her legs grow sturdy and strong. In the wild, young rhinos are sometimes seen picking up branches or other small objects and tossing them into the air.

Rhinoceroses alternate periods of eating and resting throughout the day and night but are most active in the morning and evening. Rhinos usually rest in the middle of the day, especially when the weather is warm. On the African plain, they often lie in the shade of a tree or a termite mound. Rhinos can sleep either standing up or lying down. When a rhino lies down, it bends its hind legs until it is kneeling and then lowers the rest of its body.

THE FUTURE

Wild rhinoceroses have been known to live for as long as thirty to forty years. In captivity, some rhinos have lived to be forty-five years old. With good care, rhinos like Shimba can expect to lead long, healthy lives. Most of us will never have the chance to see wild rhinoceroses, but as we watch rhinos like Shimba and her parents in zoos and animal parks, we can better appreciate how these large prehistoric-looking animals are so well suited to the wild places in which they live. Rhinos are amazing animals and reminders of what life on earth was like millions of years ago. Today and in the future, they will need the help of people to continue to survive.

46